OPEN-BOOK MANAGEMENT: GETTING STARTED

Cathy Ivancic and Jim Bado

A FIFTY-MINUTE™ SERIES BOOK

CRISP PUBLICATIONS, INC.
Menlo Park, California

OPEN-BOOK MANAGEMENT: GETTING STARTED

Cathy Ivancic and Jim Bado

CREDITS
Managing Editor: **Kathleen Barcos**
Editor: **Kay Keppler**
Production: **Leslie Power**
Typesetting: **ExecuStaff**
Cover Design: **Carol Harris**

Copyright © 1997 by Crisp Publications.

Printed in the United States of America by Bawden Printing Company.

Distribution to the U.S. Trade:

National Book Network, Inc.
4720 Boston Way
Lanham, MD 20706
1-800-462-6420

Library of Congress Catalog Card Number 97-65268
Ivancic, Cathy and Jim Bado
Open-Book Management
ISBN 1-56052-447-2

10 9 8 7 6 5 4 3 2 1

This book is printed
on recyclable paper
with soy ink.

LEARNING OBJECTIVES FOR:

OPEN-BOOK MANAGEMENT

The objectives for *Open-Book Management* are listed below. They have been developed to guide you, the reader, to the core issues covered in this book.

Objectives

❏ 1) to explain the Open-Book Management process.

❏ 2) to show how to introduce employees to company financial

❏ 3) to discuss principles and techniques of adult education.

❏ 4) to provide insights into a reward system.

Assessing Your Progress

In addition to the Learning Objectives, *Open-Book Management* includes a unique new **assessment tool*** which can be found at the back of this book. A twenty-five item, multiple choice/true-false questionnaire allows the reader to evaluate his or her comprehension of the subject matter covered. An answer sheet, with a chart matching the questions to the listed objectives, is also provided.

* Assessments should not be used in any selection process.

ABOUT THE AUTHORS

Cathy Ivancic and Jim Bado are principals of Ownership Development Inc. (ODI), which provides training and organizational-development services to build employees' skills so they can become informed, involved businesspeople.

Ivancic and Bado have more than 18 years' experience consulting with businesses to create open-book management processes and make employee ownership work. Known for their innovative learning activities, they provide companies with the tools to make learning about business concepts fun and engaging. ODI's services include:

✔ Coaching and leadership development services for initiating and sustaining a successful open-book process.

✔ Customized business education including on-site sessions and train-the-trainer approaches.

✔ Arranging visits to open-book management companies and workshops for those exploring open-book management.

For more information call or write the authors at:

Ownership Development Inc.
3198 Imrek Drive
Akron, OH 44312
(330) 896-7285 or (330) 677-1587
e-mail: 74720.1717@compuserve.com
– or –
jbado@aol.com

ABOUT THE SERIES

With over 200 titles in print, the acclaimed Crisp 50-Minute™ series presents self-paced learning at its easiest and best. These comprehensive self-study books for business or personal use are filled with exercises, activities, assessments, and case studies that capture your interest and increase your understanding.

Other Crisp products, based on the 50-Minute books, are available in a variety of learning style formats for both individual and group study, including audio, video, CD-ROM, and computer-based training.

CONTENTS

CONTENTS (continued)

A Word of Thanks

The authors wish to thank the following people for providing feedback on the initial draft of this publication: John Case, *Inc.* magazine; John Schuman, Albums, Inc.; Jay Simecek, Joseph Industries; Steve Sheppard, Foldcraft; and Randy Twyman, Fabri-Centers of America. We also want to thank our clients and friends who helped us think through the issues with open-book management and building better business people. Special thanks to Margaret Boros, Manco; Dennis Damrow, Bimba Manufacturing; Randy Dessner, Foldcraft; Art Scharinger, Floturn; Clarence Rambaud, Republic Engineered Steels, Inc.; John Warfel, James B. Oswald Co.; and Kurt Southham, Zandex Health Care Corp. for their help during the development of this book.

PREFACE

What is Open-Book Management? When you boil business to its essence, you find that companies are in business to make money. Open-book management teaches people how their companies make money. While people may work for a variety of reasons, what the company needs them to do is to help it make money. Getting employees into the action and excitement, the "ecstatic buzz," of business and teaching them their role in helping their company make money is what open-book management is all about.

As you'll learn by going through this book, open-book management isn't for corporate cowards, shrinking violets, or leaders who want to use financial information to manipulate and control people. It is, however, for companies that are interested in making more money and getting employees to act like business-people, not hired hands.

You'll also discover that open-book management isn't rocket science. It isn't a process filled with esoteric jargon and incomprehensible acronyms (at least not yet). Since it has been developed by some pioneering companies and a handful of innovative practitioners, a lot of its principles are just plain common sense. What is hard about open-book management is doing it right so that you can sustain the effort. This book will help you learn the fundamentals to get started. For the process to work, you've got to make the fundamentals fit your company's culture and business challenges.

If you're ready to learn about how to build a company of businesspeople, start by taking the quiz that follows.

Getting Started

This book is designed to help you get started with open-book management. But, before getting started, examine your own beliefs as a guide for whether this business approach makes sense. As a leader considering open-book management, which of the following do you believe are true?

T   F   Employees in this company can make a contribution to its performance.

T   F   People here deserve to share in the rewards they help create.

T   F   I can teach people what I know about the business.

T   F   People can learn about what makes the business succeed.

PREFACE (continued)

T   **F**   I don't know every way we could improve the business.

T   **F**   I would prefer to have business partners over hired hands.

T   **F**   We can grow a bigger pie of rewards if we share it.

T   **F**   Sharing information about performance has more benefits than drawbacks.

The more statements you indicated are true, the more likely your beliefs will help you in leading an open-book process. Statements you marked false indicate beliefs that will get in the way of successful implementation of open-book management.

A leader's belief that open-book management is appropriate is absolutely essential to success. If you can't envision what a successful open-book management company could look like, then nobody else can help you. On the other hand, if you believe that you can provide the outlines and then ask employees to paint the rest of the picture, your beliefs will serve you well as a leader in an open-book process.

C H A P T E R

1

Why Open
the Books?

THE ECSTATIC BUZZ OF BUSINESS

"The real voyage of discovery is not in seeking new lands,
but in seeing with new eyes!"

—Marcel Proust

While people may think that open-book management is the latest fad, some open-book management pioneers have been practicing it for more than 15 years. In fact, many successful businesses were doing it even before the term was coined. It's no fad—it's a better way of doing business.

No matter where it is practiced, open-book management has two parts: sharing financial information (opening the books) and developing a process that enables people to use business information to improve the company (management).

The definition is simple, but making it happen is complex. You can't just open the books, sit back, and watch it happen—you have to actively manage the process. You can't start passing out quarterly income statements and expect a spontaneous combustion of cost-savings and revenue-generating ideas to erupt.

For the process to succeed, you've got to do five things:

1. Share information that is relevant to employees' day-to-day jobs.

2. Build people's skills so they can understand the information.

3. Create a common vision and shared business goals.

4. Develop leaders' skills and a process where employees can use their knowledge to improve the company.

5. Design a reward system that reinforces making business improvements.

THE ECSTATIC BUZZ OF BUSINESS
(continued)

What Open-Book Management Is and Isn't

IS	ISN'T
A process that develops over time	A panacea
Hard work	The latest fad
Honest communication	Sharing only positive results
Sharing good and bad news	A right or entitlement of employees
Group responsibility for numbers	Blaming others for problems
Sharing rewards and risks	Accounting's responsibility
Believing in people	Chaos (no management)
Fun and engaging	Turning everyone into accountants
Empowering people to make decisions	Static
Tracking real-time information	A motivation "scheme"
Treating employees like adults	Sharing only quarterly financials
Focusing people on critical numbers	Group voting on all business issues
Individual responsibility	Paternalism
Having the courage to do it	Sharing all information
Employees are business people	Employees are hired hands

UNDERSTANDING WHAT YOU WANT

Before getting started with an open-book management process, it's important to think about what you want to accomplish. Why do you want to invest time and resources into the process of developing better businesspeople? What are the results you hope to achieve?

The reasons I want to open our books are: _____

_____

_____

_____

_____

The things that I want to accomplish are: _____

_____

_____

_____

_____

10 REASONS TO OPEN YOUR BOOKS

"We share everything because it helps people figure out how to improve the business. This is one reason that our stock value has increased by 1,080% in less than eight years."

—Art Scharinger, treasurer, Floturn, Inc.

Companies establish open-book management to clear away the obstacles to improved performance. Below are 10 reasons why companies open the books.

#1 To become more competitive

#2 To enhance customer service and product quality

#3 To empower a teamwork or employee-involvement effort

#4 To increase shareholder value

#5 To reduce costs and increase profits

#6 To build trust

#7 To enhance internal communication efforts

#8 To encourage individual responsibility

#9 To focus employees' actions on business challenges

#10 To create a company of winners

EMPLOYEE INVOLVEMENT IS NOT ENOUGH

One major obstacle to building an open-book management culture is fallout from previous failed efforts at employee involvement.

From the list below, check off all the programs that you have tried (or are still trying) to use to improve your company's operations. Then circle the current status of your effort.

❏ Total quality management	ALIVE	DORMANT	DEAD
❏ ISO 9000	ALIVE	DORMANT	DEAD
❏ Reengineering	ALIVE	DORMANT	DEAD
❏ Self-directed teams	ALIVE	DORMANT	DEAD
❏ Continuous improvement	ALIVE	DORMANT	DEAD
❏ Employee empowerment	ALIVE	DORMANT	DEAD
❏ Quality circles	ALIVE	DORMANT	DEAD
❏ Paradigm shift	ALIVE	DORMANT	DEAD
❏ Benchmarking	ALIVE	DORMANT	DEAD
❏ Gain sharing	ALIVE	DORMANT	DEAD
Other _____	ALIVE	DORMANT	DEAD
Other _____	ALIVE	DORMANT	DEAD
Other _____	ALIVE	DORMANT	DEAD

BUILD ON THE PAST

If yours is like most companies, you've tried a few of the initiatives on the previous page and had some success, but the effort may have fizzled over time. (If you are an exception and have one of these processes in place and working, open-book management can easily be incorporated into the system to strengthen it.)

A challenge in starting open-book management is building on the positives of previous efforts while recognizing the negatives a failed effort has left. A successful open-book management process builds on, rather than replaces, the initiatives your company has already undertaken. Open-book management is evolutionary, not revolutionary.

Use the following spaces to list the positives of previous employee involvement efforts and the negatives your company must overcome.

Positives of previous (or continuing) efforts that you can build on:

_____

_____

_____

Negatives of past efforts you want to avoid in open-book management:

_____

_____

_____

Is Your Company Ready?

Now that you've gone through the positives and negatives of previous improvement efforts, think about the current situation at your company and circle true or false to the following questions:

T   F   Most of our employees aren't interested in our business.

T   F   Sharing financial numbers will cause more problems than it will solve.

T   F   Employees will use the numbers to punish each other rather than working together.

T   F   Most employees don't have the capacity to understand our numbers.

T   F   We'll have to send people to college to understand this company.

T   F   Our accountants can never get people "real time" financial information.

T   F   SEC regulations prohibit us from sharing financial-performance information with employees.

T   F   If we share our numbers, they'll quickly get to our competitors.

MISCONCEPTIONS ABOUT OPEN-BOOK MANAGEMENT

In a successful open-book environment, the answers to all the questions on the previous page are false. If you answered true to any of them, you have identified an issue that may keep you from moving forward during the process. Read the following discussion and explore which of these issues are misconceptions and which will be key obstacles that need to be overcome to build an open-book management process at your company.

▶ *Most employees aren't interested in their company's numbers.*

Most employees never see any performance numbers, so they become apathetic about their ability to influence them. A recent survey found that 2/3 of employees reported interest in learning how their company was doing as a business. And 3/4 felt that they would work harder and smarter if they could read and understand their company's financials.

▶ *Sharing financial numbers causes more problems than it solves.*

Opening the books needs to be connected to strategic business objectives, and employees need the skills and knowledge to use the information. If done properly, understanding financial numbers will focus employees' energy on areas where they can have the greatest impact. Imagine the power of having everyone in your business—instead of a handful— concerned about and doing their best to improve cash flow, profits, or return on investment.

▶ *Employees will use the numbers to punish each other rather than working together.*

Employees must have a vehicle for working together to resolve the issues that arise from learning more about the business. This book will help you build that process at your company. In successful open-book companies, numbers are used to find areas of improvement before they become problems, instead of finding blame.

▶ *Most employees don't have the capacity to understand our numbers.*

Most employees balance a checkbook, plan for their children's college education, save for retirement and vacations, and follow a household budget. They already use the skills needed in an open-book process, they just need to learn financial language and how to apply it in their jobs.

► *We'll have to send people to college to understand this company.*

As anyone who has sat through a college-level accounting course already knows, most universities do a lousy job of teaching people about business. You won't send people to college, but you will have to do some internal education. For people to understand the business, you'll have to break down the numbers so they can see how the numbers affect their work area. You'll also have to use interactive methods and adult-learning principles to explain your business, rather than mind-numbing lectures and endless recitations of numbers.

► *Our accountants can never get people "real-time" financial information.*

You get the critical numbers you need to run the business, including cash flow, order backlog, and billable days, every day. Real-time information can be tracked by the people closest to the numbers rather than the accountants. Remember, you are not preparing audited financials to go to shareholders, you are developing a communication process for your business's critical numbers—a process that employees can use to improve the numbers on those quarterly and annual statements.

► *SEC regulations prohibit us from sharing financial performance information with employees.*

Open-book management is practiced in several successful publicly traded companies. SEC regulations do not prevent you from sharing operational numbers and department-level information with employees. You can share quarterly financials after they've been distributed to public shareholders. Some firms comply with SEC regulations by declaring everyone an insider. You may even want to consider the benefits of making employees shareholders: equity is a powerful motivator for getting employees to act like businesspeople.

► *If we share our numbers, they'll get to our competitors.*

Many privately held firms have shared their numbers without any competitive backlash, but this is a common reason for keeping your books closed. Open-book management companies take a different view of this age-old fear: they see the dangers of secrecy as more problematic than the risks of openness.

DISCLOSING FINANCIAL INFORMATION

Most leaders considering open-book management want to know what financial information is shared. How much do you need to disclose? Using the list below, check off the information you believe employees need to think like business people.

- ❏ Profit and loss (P&L) statement
- ❏ Balance sheet
- ❏ Cash-flow statement
- ❏ Operating expenses
- ❏ Cost of sales
- ❏ Gross margin
- ❏ Profit before taxes
- ❏ Billable hours
- ❏ Raw materials cost
- ❏ Selling price of products/services
- ❏ Labor cost
- ❏ Officers' salaries
- ❏ All employees salaries
- ❏ Overhead
- ❏ Average collection days
- ❏ Inventory turnover and cost
- ❏ Margin on product lines
- ❏ Individual SGA items (such as cost of phone, utilities)
- ❏ Divisional, department, or unit sales/production numbers

THE DISCLOSURE DILEMMA: THE COMPETITION

Before thinking about how disclosure will affect your competitive position, consider your competitors. Complete this page thinking about the firms that are your direct competitors.

Check all of the following that you know about your competition:

- ❏ Pricing policies

- ❏ Marketing strategy/territory

- ❏ Overhead costs

- ❏ Fringe benefits offered to employees

- ❏ General wage and salary levels

- ❏ General trends in profitability

- ❏ Margins on products/services

- ❏ Range of production capabilities/services offered

- ❏ Weaknesses as a company

- ❏ Major customers

- ❏ Order backlog

- ❏ Strengths as a company

- ❏ Stock value

- ❏ Sales volume

Now, return to the list and check any items that you could make a good guess about—even though you are not privy to the details. Corporate leaders with any business savvy can guess fairly accurately what their competitors' numbers look like.

> **If you can guess what your competitors' numbers are, they can guess what yours are.**

YOUR FIRM'S SENSITIVE INFORMATION

If disclosure to the competition is one of the major obstacles to opening your books, answer the following questions.

What information *absolutely* must be kept from your competitors? Be specific. Consider dollar amount on project bids, new research underway, and pricing on particular products or services.

_____

_____

Certain people in your company know this information. List the reasons why these people do not share the sensitive information with the competition.

_____

_____

If employees knew this information, why would they be any different from the people who already know it?

_____

_____

Concern about information falling into the hands of the competition is usually rooted in the following assumptions:

1. Employees cannot understand how the business works

2. Employees cannot be trusted with the information

Open-book management companies reject both these assumptions. However, they recognize that these assumptions are obstacles to be overcome. Trust and business knowledge grow gradually with an open-book process. As people become more aware of how the business makes money, they are better equipped to safeguard the information with the same vigor as those who know it now.

SHARING THE INFORMATION

Open-book management is similar to the quality and customer service movements. The quality movement took information and responsibility for quality out of the engineering department and shared it with operators; the customer-service movement has dispersed sales and customer-service information (and responsibility) to everyone in the company. The driving force behind those initiatives was to give employees closest to the customer all the information they needed to produce the highest quality product and to generate the best customer service.

When you open the books, you share information formerly reserved for top-level leaders and the accounting department. The same principle applies: the information shared is what is needed to improve the business. At highly developed open-book companies, that means sharing virtually all financial information—with the exception of individual salaries.

But sharing everything isn't where most companies start. The open-book management process is a road that ultimately leads to full disclosure. As you travel this road, you build employees' trust, skills, and knowledge.

BOOKS CRACKED OPEN	BOOKS ARE OPEN
Limited Information Sharing	**Total Information Sharing**
• Inform people of strategic goals	• Employees help develop goals
• Announce financial results orally	• Share written information with all
• Share information with leadership group only	• Widespread information sharing
• Provide written summary data	• Line item data from P&L
• Give people income statement	• Full financials with line items

Companies start somewhere at the beginning of the road (left-hand column) and move toward full disclosure. How quickly they progress depends on leadership initiative, how fast people's skills develop, and employees' interest in learning about the business.

16

THE OPEN-BOOK MANAGEMENT PUZZLE

An open-book management process includes five elements that work together to create an environment where employees can think and act like business people.

1) **Shared vision based on business goals**

2) **Credible communication about financial information**

3) **Business knowledge of critical numbers**

4) **Leadership skills and processes to make it work**

5) **Rewards for success**

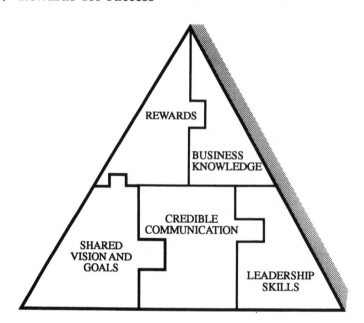

The three puzzle pieces on the bottom form the foundation for your open-book management effort and support the pieces on top. What holds the pieces together is leadership commitment to the process and trust among the employees of the numbers and each others' intentions.

> **The best early advice we can give you is . . . GET STARTED!**

Ideas for Getting Started

- Begin the planning process for opening the books.

- Survey your employees' understanding of business concepts and critical numbers.

- Hold an initial session for leaders on open-book management concepts and principles.

- Start posting financial results in a graphic form where employees can see them.

- Stop giving annual pay increases and start a system of variable pay.

- Pass out a simplified income statement.

- Hold a fun, understandable training session on business concepts.

- Run a pilot in a department or division (especially if you're a big company).

Companies get started in different ways depending on their history, employees' and leaders' skill level, and business needs. Working through the rest of this book will help you identify how to get started with open-book management.

C H A P T E R

2

Critical Numbers and Business Goals

WHAT ARE CRITICAL NUMBERS?

"It [open-book management] transforms human behavior . . . It connects every workerwith the ecstatic buzz of business and enables ordinary people to perform better than anyone ever expected."

—Inc.

When you think about opening your books, you're considering a process that will educate people about how your company makes money. Through it, employees will learn the crucial role that they play in helping the company make money. Open-book companies use their communication process to focus employees on "critical numbers." What is a critical number?

A critical number is something that is essential to your business's success. It could be related to increasing revenues, decreasing costs, improving margins, reducing outstanding debt, or generating cash flow. It is a number that employees can measure and track against a plan, targets, or previous performance.

Critical numbers are:

- Essential to your business's success

- Measurable and trackable

- Area(s) where employee energy needs to be concentrated

- Something that can be affected by employees at their job site

- A focal point for improvement

Based on where your business stands today, what are three critical numbers all employees should understand and track?

1. _____

2. _____

3. _____

> **If you're having a hard time defining your company's critical numbers, review the reasons you cited for opening your books in Chapter 1. They will indicate where you need to focus.**

WHAT ARE CRITICAL NUMBERS?
(continued)

Examples of Critical Numbers

Critical numbers vary from business to business and change depending on business conditions and strategic goals.

Company-wide critical numbers may include the following:

- Operating income
- Gross margin
- Inventory turns
- Billable hours/days/order backlog
- Cash flow
- Net revenues (daily, weekly, monthly)

- Cost of sales/cost of goods sold
- Scrap rate/customer returns
- Days receivable
- Debt repayment
- Customer-service measures

These factors are all important in determining a company's health. It is impossible, however, for employees to monitor all of these at the same time. Open-book companies pick two or three companywide numbers that represent current goals and use their communication and education processes to link the companywide numbers to the local numbers that employees monitor in their work. Below are three examples of critical numbers in action.

▶ *Operating margin and cost reduction*

A mature manufacturing firm identified operating margin as one of its critical numbers. Employees focused on things they could do in their workday to reduce the company's operating costs, hence improving margin.

▶ *Occupancy rate and breakeven*

A hotel used occupancy rate as a critical number. Employees were educated about the hotel's breakeven point (the number of rooms that needed to be filled each night to cover all operating costs) and provided with real-time information on occupancy rate.

► *Billable costs*

A professional engineering company used billable costs to help people think about how the company pays for expenses associated with a project. It began tracking items like photocopies, phone calls, and overnight packages that should have been, but weren't, billed to clients.

Critical Numbers Change with Business Changes

Bottom-Line-Bob's Experience

Bob had always considered himself a bottom-line oriented manager. In his 10 years as a manager for a medium-sized metal fabricating plant, he had focused on pretax profit rather than gross sales dollars as some of his counterparts did. A recordbreaking profitable quarter also produced many shipping delays, which eroded the customer base. Even though Bob's critical number—pretax profit—was right on target for the year, something was terribly wrong.

Bob pulled his team of managers together, and they started to track another critical number: on-time delivery. Bob and his managers took the word to employees in each department. Workers were asked to identify the factors that contribute to on-time delivery. By looking at what caused delays and what contributed to prompt execution, employees identified what their teams needed to assure on-time delivery. Workers developed measures that focused on their contribution to the new critical number. With employees working toward reaching their targets, delivery times improved steadily over the next several months.

TRACKING CRITICAL NUMBERS

Most people track information related to their jobs. A sales representative may track orders booked, profit margin on sales, or sales dollars; a collections clerk may count accounts settled, dollars collected, or bad-debt dollars; and a production worker may know units produced, returns of units, and down-time on a machine.

Most people track something in their job, but do not normally think of it as related to financial performance. Helping employees discover and understand their key indicator or critical number and relating it to financial performance is a key function of leaders throughout an open-book company.

On the left, list the companywide critical numbers you have already identified. These numbers tell you if the business is on track. On the right, list job-level indicators of performance, the things employees track or should track. (There are more than one for each company indicator.)

COMPANYWIDE INDICATORS

1. _____

2. _____

3. _____

JOB-LEVEL INDICATORS

1. _____
   _____

2. _____
   _____

3. _____
   _____

What are the connections between the two lists? As a leader you must help employees find the connections between these two lists (at the beginning you may need to make the connection for them). Initiating a discussion about the connections is what drives improvements in an open-book management company.

Do You Know Your Critical Number?

Randy, who works in the laminating department of a seating manufacturer, can answer that question in the blink of an eye. "We want to get the Dura-edge panel through the shop in four days," he says. "If we can do that, then we limit the amount of overtime and get the product to the customer on time." Dura-edge is a laminated panel that has been delayed as it moves through the shop.

A committee in Randy's department is charged with initiating the effort to move the Dura-edge more quickly through the shop. The committee meets for a half-hour twice a week to work on this problem.

However, that does not mean that the laminating department is responsible for the ultimate solution. In last week's meeting, the committee brought in some people from the next department. The group found that these panels were often set aside until they had several to run at one time. The Dura-edge needs to move through the shop steadily because it takes more processing than other panels. "Now," Randy says, "they see that they've got to jump on them right away to get them out in four days."

Do they care if it goes out in four days? "Some people still don't care or get mad when we try to do things differently. But we've got the responsibility of explaining to them that [the reward] is there for the taking. All we have to do is make it happen," says Randy. Randy and his coworkers know that they have a direct effect on the gains part of the bonus formula. When they move the Dura-edge to four days in the shop, they reduce overtime hours.

Before moving to open-book management, people did not know how overtime affected their company. Some employees were working as much as 60 hours a week. Now employees are trying to maintain a 40-hour work week. The goal for the plant is to have 5% or less overtime across the board. Cutting overtime hours helps move everyone a little closer to getting the added part of the bonus and helps get the product to the customer on time.

Do You Know Your Critical Number? (continued)

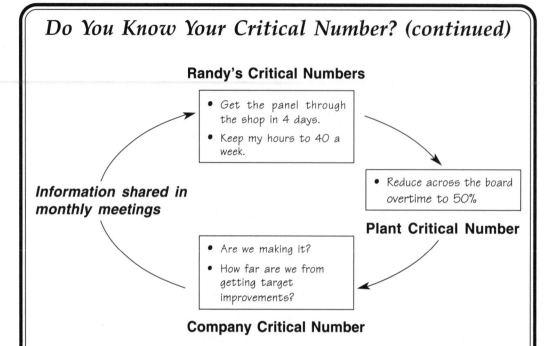

Randy's Critical Numbers

- Get the panel through the shop in 4 days.
- Keep my hours to 40 a week.

- Reduce across the board overtime to 50%

Plant Critical Number

Information shared in monthly meetings

- Are we making it?
- How far are we from getting target improvements?

Company Critical Number

The "four days" target enables employees to watch their own critical number on a daily basis. Weekly, they work on specific problems in committee to improve the number. At a monthly company meeting, they get the overall results compared to the plan. It is here where people see how their work has affected the company's performance and ultimately their pocketbooks. That's where employees see how their work affects the corporate financials and find out if they are making it or not making it.

When asked about the next steps for the Dura-edge committee Randy replied, "Get it to three days!"

CREATE A "LINE OF SIGHT"

Employees do things every day that affect the performance of their companies. To act like business people, employees need to see the link from their work to the company's overall critical numbers. Building broader understanding of this line of sight from daily work to the company's financial statements helps employees act like businesspeople.

Imagine that a factory worker needs to decide whether to rework a slightly damaged part or pull a new part off the shelf. If the worker knows how the cost of the new part and the costs associated with the rework of the old part (labor and overhead) will affect the company's performance, he or she can make an informed decision. Without that overview, the cost information represents a seemingly arbitrary target set by a supervisor. With the line-of sight connection, the cost information is a tool for self-improvement and making a savvy business decision.

NEXT YEAR'S CRITICAL NUMBERS

A critical number is only meaningful if employees have something to compare it to. You can start by comparing it to previous performance to explain this year's future. Projecting critical numbers helps open-book companies set targets for performance.

Target setting begins with the companywide critical numbers and works backwards. Your objective is to uncover the line-of-sight connections that show people how they contribute to the companywide numbers.

Take one of the critical numbers that you identified earlier in this chapter and trace the line of sight backwards to the individual. Use the spaces below to set subtargets (measures) for the critical number. First identify where you are this year, and then use the right-hand column to project where the number ought to be next year.

	MEASURE	CURRENT PERFORMANCE	NEXT YEAR'S TARGET
Companywide	_____	_____	_____
Plant/division	_____	_____	_____
Department/team	_____	_____	_____
Individual	_____	_____	_____

Did you find it more difficult to set the targets as you moved away from your job? If you did, you can see why the planning process is a group activity. If you found it easy to set targets, consider whether people in other parts of the organization will buy into your targets or believe that you can set realistic goals in their areas.

RELAY REAL-TIME INFORMATION

"It takes our accountants at least a month to close the books.
There is no way we can get people real-time information.
We just aren't set up that way!"

—Manager starting an open-book process

People need real-time information to measure whether they are hitting targets in their area. When managers think of building a system of real-time information, they commonly think of overhauling the accounting function or building an elaborate computer program to handle the data. Just imagine how busy the accountants will be with the enormous task of identifying all the critical numbers employees should watch and giving each of them feedback each day on how they affect it!

Even if the company's leadership could accomplish this gargantuan task, they would still fail in creating an effective open-book process. Why? Because the leadership still owns the performance numbers. Accounting will not initiate two-way communication, create a setting for telling individual stories about performance, or build broader responsibility for the numbers. The best place to start developing real-time information is with each person's job. It starts with questions.

► *What are the critical numbers you follow in your job?*

► *How do those numbers connect to our department or team's performance numbers?*

► *How does that number affect the plant/division and the company's performance?*

► *What should these numbers be next quarter, next month, next week?*

► *Are you watching the numbers that will help you reach your vision of the future?*

> **Ask yourself the questions above and then ask the people you work with the same questions. Tracking and planning helps people take ownership of the numbers.**

START (OR RESTART) THE PLANNING

Here are some of the ways that companies jump-start their planning.

✔ **Give people targets in the beginning.**

If no one has done forecasting, you will have to give people initial targets. Pick target numbers at the job-level that relate to company-wide critical numbers. After a reasonable period of tracking, ask people if the targets are realistic.

✔ **Establish a cross-functional implementation team.**

The team identifies critical numbers and establishes a continuous planning cycle.

✔ **Dust off your budget.**

If your critical numbers are tied to costs, you may be able to use your budget as a mechanism for talking about how each department's budget contributes to companywide critical numbers.

✔ **Make targets the content of your huddle-based communication process.**

In the main huddle (leadership group), identify and track the departmental/divisional numbers that affect the companywide critical numbers. In the minihuddles, identify and track the team and individual numbers that affect those departmental numbers.

✔ **Forecast each line of the financial statement.**

Track your progress against each item on a quarterly, monthly, or weekly basis. Some firms put people in charge of monitoring specific lines, and they compile the results together in their companywide huddle.

Planning: An Investment that Pays

"We were always a company that shared a lot of information," said the president of an open-book insurance company. "The big improvements came for us when we started involving a large part of the company in planning." Eight years ago the company decided it needed to get everybody "on the same page." It now regularly holds semiannual one- or two-day off-site planning sessions, hiring an outside facilitator to keep meetings on track, and involving about one-third of the company's employees (officers through mid-level leaders).

A leader's job is to bring the results back to employees in his department. The planning process—part relationship building and part strategic planning—is a substantial investment for the company, but worth the time and effort. According to the company president, "When we don't get that opportunity to plan, that's when we really pay for it." People feel left out, the rumor mill takes over, and people develop their own (sometimes competing) priorities.

SHE NEEDS TO OPEN THE PLANNING PROCESS

CONNECTING CRITICAL NUMBERS TO GOALS

"I never hit a golf shot I couldn't imagine first."

—Jack Nicklaus

If you want to make something new happen, you must be able to envision it first. Jack Nicklaus can imagine the 20-foot putt plopping into the hole, pull out his putter, and make it happen, but in business it takes a group of people to sink the shot.

Employees in an open-book management effort need to be able to imagine where the company is going and how their increasing knowledge will help get it there. In an open-book company, the vision is anchored in concrete business goals based on critical numbers that tie the whole process together.

If your company already has a vision statement, start with that. If it doesn't, start by writing one yourself and getting other leaders in your company to comment, critique, and add their ideas to it. Don't stop with leaders. Eventually, to get their support, employees need to be part of this conversation, too.

Your Vision for the Company

The exercise below will get you started in establishing a vision. If you already have a vision statement, do this exercise, then compare your statement with what you write here.

What do you envision your company to be like in five years?

_____

_____

_____

_____

How big will it be (sales/employees)? _____

What will its critical numbers look like? _____

_____

_____

What problems have been eliminated? _____

_____

_____

What will it feel like to work at the company? _____

_____

_____

What milestones have been accomplished? _____

_____

_____

What new challenges are you taking on? _____

_____

_____

If you found this exercise difficult, you are not alone. Most people have not practiced dreaming about the future. This is especially true of nonexecutives. This "vision deficit" is an obstacle to be overcome; people can't help you make the vision a reality unless they can see it in their own heads.

If you haven't already, it is time to discover what other people in your company think about the firm's future. As you discuss their ideas, you may find that your own vision of the future changes.

YOU CAN'T DO IT ALONE

Improving your company is a team effort. Managers and informal leaders need to join you in building the vision for how open-book management will help you attain your goals.

How far along are they in their understanding today? Rate your company by circling a number under the following questions.

What percentage of company management could describe your company's vision?

0%   10%   20%   30%   40%   50%   60%   70%   80%   90%   100%

How many could tell you what this year's corporate goals are?

0%   10%   20%   30%   40%   50%   60%   70%   80%   90%   100%

What percentage would identify the same critical numbers as you do?

0%   10%   20%   30%   40%   50%   60%   70%   80%   90%   100%

How do you know that you circled the right percentages in answering these questions?

_____

_____

_____

_____

As a leader, it is often difficult to get accurate feedback, especially when people think that their answers will affect their status (such as promotions or bonuses) with the company. Think about the obstacles to checking your perceptions, and use the spaces below to list five ways to get accurate feedback about your answers.

1. _____

_____

_____

2. _____

_____

_____

3. _____

_____

_____

4. _____

_____

_____

5. _____

_____

_____

To help yourself get better feedback, implement at least two of the things you have listed. Checking your perceptions will help you determine how much of your energy needs to be spent on building a common vision among your leadership group.

TAKING THE VISION TO THE EMPLOYEES

In addition to mobilizing your company's leadership, you must find ways to bring the vision to employees. Companies that have built a shared vision get employees at all levels involved in imagining the future. An ideal way for employees to become committed to a future state is to provide opportunities for them to help create and implement it. Below are some ideas (big and small) for starting the process.

▶ Ask a focus group questions about where the company is going. Use their answers to understand how much of the vision is shared.

▶ Provide reading materials on open-book management (such as this book) to other leaders and ask them to comment on how it fits with your company's future.

▶ Develop a task force of "champions" who will identify the obstacles to the vision and help plan a strategy for overcoming them.

▶ Hold an introductory open-book management workshop for leaders that challenges them to dream about the future.

▶ Have employees in each work area identify how they can help take the company toward its vision.

▶ Ask small groups of employees to read the company's vision and comment on what will prevent its achievement.

▶ Develop and distribute a written survey that asks employees where the company is going and publish the results for all to see.

BRING YOUR CRITICAL NUMBERS INTO FOCUS

Clarifying a common vision helps you to identify which objectives are priorities. Critical numbers need to change as you bring your objectives into focus. Consider the following companies:

An auto parts manufacturer initially identified only one critical number: net income. After analyzing their group vision of the future, management added customer-service measures and started tracking product diversification to monitor progress toward long-term goals.

By discussing obstacles to achieving their mission, a service firm identified excessive absenteeism as a key barrier to attaining its ideal future state. Absences were picked as a companywide critical number for everyone to watch.

Leaders at a highly leveraged firm found that cash flow for debt repayment was a critical number, but after considering their vision, they also started monitoring capital improvements to move the company toward where they wanted to be in five years.

Look at the numbers that you have identified as companywide critical numbers. Now that you have thought more about where you are headed in developing open-book management, what critical numbers help you track your progress toward reaching your company's vision? Use the space on the right to note how you will modify your companywide critical numbers to ensure that they help you reach your vision.

CRITICAL NUMBERS	MODIFY? HOW?
1. _____	_____
2. _____	_____
3. _____	_____

CHAPTER 3

Prepare to Open the Books

GETTING THE WORD OUT

"In a parade, everyone has sheet music. . . . I've never seen a parade yet that was very impressive with only the drum major with the sheet music. That's what we're doing here [with open-book management]. And if you do that, you unleash the power of 145 people thinking about a common goal."

—Bob Argabright, Chesapeake Packaging Co. in
Open-Book Management, by John Case, 1996

Successful open-book management is more than just sending employees financial statements. It requires continuous two-way communication about the company's performance. The credibility of that communication to individual employees—and employees using that information to improve performance—is the heart that pumps life into an open-book process.

As in a marching band, each musician has individual sheet music (job-level critical numbers) to understand how each instrument contributes to the group's success. Just like musicians, employees need opportunities to practice their skills together to make it work. Strengthening your company's ability to communicate about company performance is a key to successful open-book management.

What Is the Current Method?

List the top five ways people in your company communicate about how the company is doing. Remember to include written and verbal information, meetings, activities, and—of course—informal means of communication.

1. _____

2. _____

3. _____

4. _____

5. _____

> **Did you include the rumor mill?**

RATE YOUR APPROACH

The following is a list of elements of effective communication about performance. Using the list on the previous page as a guide, rate your company's overall approach to communicating about performance.

	NEVER	ALMOST NEVER	SOMETIMES	ALMOST ALWAYS	ALWAYS
Includes the numbers and stories behind the numbers	1	2	3	4	5
Two-way communication	1	2	3	4	5
Understood by employees	1	2	3	4	5
Runs on a regular schedule	1	2	3	4	5
Linked to what people do in their jobs	1	2	3	4	5
Allows people to describe their contribution to performance	1	2	3	4	5
Fun and engaging	1	2	3	4	5
Connected to rewards	1	2	3	4	5

Add up all the responses to the self-quiz. If you scored:

20 points or less: Your company may be sharing information about performance, but you are probably sharing financial results using traditional approaches.

21–34 points: You are making some efforts to make communication about performance part of everyday work. The items you rated lower identify opportunities to improve communication about performance.

35 points or more: Your company has developed a two-way communication process. You should concentrate on rewards, leadership skills, employee knowledge, and developing shared goals to enhance the effectiveness of your communication.

NEW WAYS TO SHARE INFORMATION

In most companies, managers and employees wait for the financial data to be brought down from the financial experts like sacred scrolls from the elders. After a month—or sometimes several months—a team or department will get results on how well they performed. The information is usually summarized, so one can only guess what the individual contribution has been to performance. This traditional approach is very different from an open-book process, where two-way communication is based on real-time information.

Traditional Financial Communication	Effective Open-Book Process
• Delayed information	• Real-time numbers
• Top-down	• Two-way closed circle
• Summarized (not specific)	• Specific and detailed
• Stories told by top-level leaders	• Stories told by those closest to action
• Often a special event	• Regular and routine
• Designed for outsiders, such as bankers or investors	• Designed for insiders

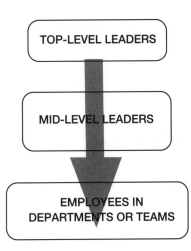

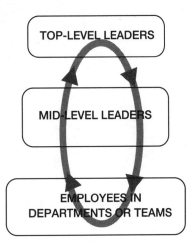

GAMES, HUDDLES, TEAMS, AND SCORECARDS

Successful open-book management companies use many communication methods, including newsletters, bulletin boards, suggestion boxes, annual dinners, employee celebrations, e-mail, and even the traditional payroll stuffer. They also will have a well-developed process for tracking and sharing real-time information.

Many open-book management companies use face-to-face meetings—often called "huddles"—where employees track and report their own performance compared to planned performance and their own projections. Making this sharing of information into a game—complete with prizes and rewards for outstanding performance—helps break through some of the reservations people have about learning financial concepts.

At the team or department level, employees share their numbers and stories in a meeting, a minihuddle, in preparation for the main huddle, where leaders use this information to build company- or plantwide financial statements for the period. The company's scorecard—the financial results—come back to employees in a minihuddle where leaders help employees understand and interpret how their work affected those numbers.

An example of huddle-based communication

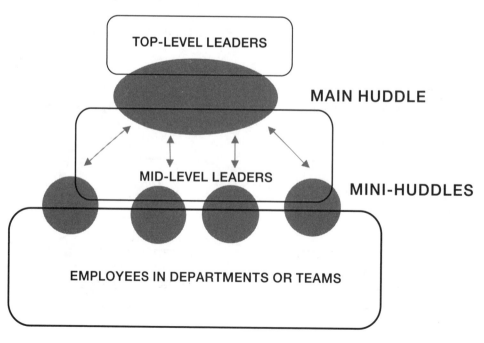

HAVE A LITTLE FUN

Even though the financial results of your company are serious business, the methods you use to communicate them don't need to be overly serious. Let's face it: when most companies talk about performance, they can make even the most outstanding results seem dull and uneventful.

Our traditional methods of communicating about performance are designed for outsiders, not insiders. Insiders find the information credible because they see its connection to their work lives, not from the serious way you present it.

> **Making money is fun! Reaching your goals is fun! Your methods of communication need to reflect that spirit.**

Celebrate the Milestones

How do people at your company have fun? Think about the rituals and activities that mark celebrations: birthdays, promotions, sports events, holidays, graduations, births, and even home purchases. List below the things people in your company do when they celebrate milestones and victories in their lives.

_____

_____

_____

Which of these can be done at work to celebrate performance?

_____

_____

_____

8 IDEAS FOR INVOLVEMENT

#1 **Create opportunities for small wins.** It's no fun if you never win. Your companywide objective may be to maintain a cash flow that is twice today's figure, but you can set more achievable hurdles tied to reducing inventory or improving collections.

#2 **Celebrate every win with gusto!** There is no rule that says you can't make noise, sing, eat, wave flags, throw your hat up in the air, jump up on your chair, and even dance when you hit your goals.

#3 **Make props and visual aids.** While your banker may not appreciate your tracking monthly cash flow as a 10-foot bucket on the wall, employees will grow to understand the concept faster if you make it visual.

#4 **Keep track the way you would for competitive sports.** You never hear the announcer at a football game say, "On page 6 of the handout you will see the detailed graph that shows Central High has improved yards gained in the second quarter." Keep score on a big board where everyone can see it, and provide some high-energy commentary to explain the results.

#5 **Give employees a chance to do their own play-by-play.** Half of the fun in watching a sports event is giving your own interpretations. It is always more fun to figure out what is happening on your own than take the word of the commentators. Most of us want to see the slow-motion replay ourselves. Allow employees the time and a forum to call the action as they see it. Keep an open mind . . . you may hear some great ideas.

#6 **Develop the spirit of competition and keep it focused where it should be.** Stay focused on your overall financial goals. Rather than competing against other departments or coworkers, employees in open-book companies are focused on industry benchmarks, last-year's results, the annual plan, or that period's forecast.

#7 **Play small games that engage employees.** If the president of the company regularly gives five bucks to the first employee who can tell him what last month's gross profit margin was, people will pay attention.

#8 **Park your inhibitions and use your creativity.** It's fun, interesting, and engaging when the chief financial officer presents the monthly results in a rap song; even if he is a bit undignified. If you're worried about what people will think, perhaps you should worry more about how dangerous it is when people don't think.

C H A P T E R

4

Developing Employees as Businesspeople

CONFRONTING COMMON MYTHS

"[Open-book management] methods offer hope that workers in even the most mundane jobs can be inspired to boost their companies' wealth—and, by doing so, their own."

—Los Angeles Times

It is ironic that people spend most of their lives working, but do not understand how their company makes money. Of course, in the absence of facts, myths and rumors arise. These myths are an obstacle to developing better businesspeople. Check off the common myths that you think employees believe about your business.

- ❏ You have to cheat to be successful in business.
- ❏ Businesses can charge whatever they want for their products.
- ❏ The company keeps its profits in a bank account.
- ❏ Our business is too complex to understand.
- ❏ Anybody with a good idea can make it in business.
- ❏ Our company makes money hand-over-fist.
- ❏ Our leaders always pay themselves extravagant bonuses.
- ❏ It's immoral to make a lot of money.
- ❏ So what if there are expenses, they're all write-offs anyway.
- ❏ All business people care about is making money.
- ❏ Our profit is at least 50% of sales.
- ❏ Good employees do only what they're told to do.
- ❏ There's no reason to change, since we've been successful for 30 years doing it that way.
- ❏ All stockholders are interested in are this quarter's earnings.

Use this list to check your perceptions with other leaders and employees at your company. Understanding which myths are believed will help you focus educational efforts on addressing people's concerns that come from these beliefs.

WHY EMPLOYEES WANT TO LEARN ABOUT THE BUSINESS

To learn something new, we all need to be motivated. Use the spaces below to write down five things that might motivate your employees to learn more about the business. What do you think they want to know? What questions interest them?

1. _____

_____

2. _____

_____

3. _____

_____

4. _____

_____

5. _____

_____

21 Things Employees Learn by Understanding Their Company's Financial Performance

1. Whether the company is profitable
2. How much cash the company has
3. How the company is performing in the marketplace
4. Whether their own job is secure
5. Who the company owes money to
6. How much cash is invested in inventory
7. Whether the company's customers pay their bills
8. If the company pays its suppliers
9. How their company compares to the competition
10. How they are doing on the bonus/gain-sharing formula
11. What the company's assets would be worth if they were sold
12. The total amount of the bank loan
13. How the company's new product line is performing
14. How much scrap employees produce
15. How much the company owes to its employees
16. How this year's sales are compared to last year's
17. If the company is meeting its business plan
18. If their department is hitting its financial goals
19. If profits are up or down compared to last year
20. A better understanding of their company
21. A better understanding of business

"HOT TOPICS" CAN MOTIVATE EMPLOYEES

For some people, the opportunity to learn about the company and build their own skills are powerful motivators.

Another motivator for employees can be learning about the latest "hot topic" (that is, something happening in your business that people are curious about and discussing on their own time).

You can help motivate people to learn by integrating a hot topic into your business-education process. Use the spaces below to write down what people are discussing around the water cooler or the latest business-related rumor to run through your facility.

1. _____

2. _____

3. _____

Examples of "Hot Topics"

- Launching a product line
- New competitor entering the marketplace
- Issuing of dividends
- Change in benefits
- Altering a business strategy (for example, marketing)
- Company restructuring/reengineering
- Major change in sales/costs/profits
- Acquisition, divestiture, or new subsidiary
- Rumor of a "bad quarter"
- Issuing bonus checks

Addressing a hot topic as part of your training will catch people's attention. But remember, it's hot, so don't get burned: be clear to employees why you are including the hot topic in your training (for example, discussion or illustration, not resolution or decision).

CONQUERING NUMBER PHOBIA

Let's face it; many people don't like numbers. Maybe they had a bad experience back in grammar school (flash-card phobia), they never learned how to calculate common functions like percentages, or their skills have gotten rusty from disuse.

As a leader, your job is to create an environment where people can conquer math anxiety and think and act like businesspeople. Check all the following statements that apply to your employees' views of numbers and receiving company financial information.

- ❏ Financial statements have too many numbers; you can't tell what's important.

- ❏ Terms on statements are written by accountants for accountants.

- ❏ I never did like going to math class.

- ❏ Financial experts speak in accounting gibberish.

- ❏ Taking care of the money is my spouse's job.

- ❏ My eyes glaze over when I look at a list of numbers.

- ❏ Even if I understood the statements, they wouldn't tell me anything.

- ❏ This company will never share real financial information.

- ❏ Our company has two sets of books.

- ❏ My accountant takes care of all my personal finances.

- ❏ No one ever sees the numbers where I work.

- ❏ It isn't important for me to understand financial statements.

- ❏ I can't figure out tips at restaurants.

- ❏ So what if I understand them; I can't use the information anyway.

- ❏ Accounting reality doesn't reflect business reality.

- ❏ When I look at the statements, I can't tell how I affect the bottom line.

You can check the accuracy of your perceptions through a focus group, polling your open-book management task force, or talking with employees. You may find that you need to start by teaching people basic math skills or integrating it into your overall approach to business education.

TEACH BUSINESS CONCEPTS WITH REAL-LIFE EXAMPLES

Most people use business concepts in their daily activities. The problem is that most companies ask employees to leave their personal experiences, and often their brains, at the door when they punch the time clock. Open-book management unlocks the knowledge and experience of employees to improve the business.

While number phobia may be rampant, it is not because people lack the ability to understand numbers and how a business works. Today's average employee is the most educated worker in history. The average person knows more about health care than the average doctor did at the turn of the century. Most people think nothing of treating their child's fever or medicating their persistent cough.

People have a similar education in managing a household. On a regular basis, a company's employees wrestle with complex financial decisions like allocating resources for a household budget, planning for their children's education, and directing savings for retirement. Even if all they do is occasionally balance their checkbook or pay off their credit cards, they use business concepts.

Most people also keep track of personal critical numbers—whether it's a win-loss ratio of their favorite team, their cholesterol count, or the performance of their retirement investments. They have the fundamental knowledge; the challenge is to transfer that personal experience to the world of business. A simple and understandable way to start a business education is to start with personal examples and then relate the real-life concepts to the real-world of your business.

> **It's up to you to begin the process of conquering number phobia**

A REAL-LIFE ANALOGY

Most of us have experience running a household. Think of a moment about which financial measures are important to running it. Where do you get your money (sources) and how do you spend it (uses)?

An Example of Household Sources and Uses of Cash

GET	SPEND
Paycheck	Groceries
Spouse's paycheck	Utilities
Interest on bank account	Mortgage payment
Borrowed from family/friend	Household maintenance/repair
Borrowed from bank	Car payment/lease
Garage sale/hobby	Car maintenance/gas
Credit card (charge for it)	Savings for retirement
	Insurance
	College fund
	Credit card payment
	Clothing/dry cleaning/laundry
	Personal grooming
	Entertainment
	Medical bills

If you're like most people, you have more uses for your money than sources of funds; and it wouldn't be hard to list another 20 expense items the household spends its money on. The same is true for your business.

COMPARING HOUSEHOLD TO BUSINESS FINANCES

As individuals we may use a notebook, a computer program, our checkbook, or some other method to keep track of our money and what we spend it on (for some people it's that drawer where they keep all the receipts).

Businesses use financial statements such as the balance sheet and profit and loss (P&L) income statements to monitor how the company performs. Unfortunately, many leaders forget how challenging it can be for an employee to read a financial statement. Most nonfinancial people will be intimidated by the long list of numbers on these statements.

Business financials, however, record many of the same financial concepts used in personal life. A balance sheet like the one below can be developed from a personal life example.

Personal Balance Sheet

MARVIN FRISBINE HOUSEHOLD
December 31, 1997

Assets		Liabilities and Equity	
Checking and savings accounts	2,723	Amount owed on credit cards	5,660
Purchased groceries and supplies	123	Monthly mortgage and car payments	1,450
Prepaid insurance (car and house)	375	Utilities owed	191
		Amount owed for roof repair	3,500
		Total amount still owed on car	11,220
IRA	30,000	Total amount still owed on house	78,640
Car	17,500	Equity	
House	100,000	Mortgage and auto loans (repaid)	27,460
Furniture	7,400	Retirement funds saved retained	30,000
Total assets	158,121	Total liabilities and equity	158,121

COMPARING BUSINESS AND HOUSEHOLD TERMS

Businesses use different terms to describe many of the same things we're doing in our personal lives. From the balance sheet on the previous page, try to match the business balance sheet term listed in the left-hand column with its equivalent from the personal balance sheet.

BUSINESS TERM	PERSONAL-LIFE TERM
Cash	_____
Inventory	_____
Prepaid insurance	_____
Machinery and equipment	_____
Fixed assets	_____
Other investments	_____
Short-term debt	_____
Accounts payable	_____
Accrued expenses	_____
Long-term debt	_____
Equity	_____
Retained earnings	_____

After filling in the list, you can see that your employees already use many business terms to describe their households. A key to understanding how a business operates is understanding the accountant's language.

Similar examples can be drawn between the P&L and cash-flow statements and household income and household spending of cash.

3 REAL-LIFE ANALOGIES YOU CAN USE

(BALANCE SHEET)

Draw two boxes as shown (one for assets, one for liabilities and equity). Ask people to list all the things that they own (assets) and all the bills they owe (liabilities). Have them list short- and long-term obligations and credit cards. For equity, use their house's value and the amount still owed on the mortgage as an example. Once the list is completed, ask:

► How do they balance short- and long-term obligations?

► How do they decide which bills are a priority?

► Have they ever sold an asset (like a car), and what value did they realize for it?

YOUR ASSETS	COMPANY'S ASSETS

After the personal list is built, ask people to think about what the business owns and what it owes. Compare that list to their personal one and the company's balance sheet.

Question to make it fun: Is that exercise equipment you own, but don't use, an asset or a liability?

(PROFIT AND LOSS)

Draw another grid and ask people to think about last month. Ask them where they got money from (revenues/sales) and what they spent it on (expenses/taxes). Build a list of the items they generate. Once it's completed, ask questions like:

► How often do you spend money on this item?

► Is this something related to running your household or not?

► What do you do when household expenses exceed revenues?

► How often do you pay city, state, and federal taxes?

► If you have money left over after expenses, who decides how it is spent?

YOUR INCOME/EXPENSES	COMPANY'S INCOME/EXPENSES

Now do the same thing for the business. Compare this list to their personal list and the company's P&L statement.

Question to make it fun: Is alimony a revenue or expense?

3 REAL-LIFE ANALOGIES YOU CAN USE (continued)

CASH-FLOW STATEMENT

Using another grid, ask people to think about one day and where they get cash and how they spend it. Include everything—gas, lunch, newspaper, pop, milk, groceries—whatever. Attach a dollar value to each item and flowchart the day. Ask questions like:

► How much money did you need?

► Are there any ways to stretch the cash you have?

► How do you plan for cash?

► Why wouldn't you spend cash for something?

► Do you incur expenses daily that you pay for monthly (for example, cable, electric)? How do you keep track of them?

► If you went to the convenience store and didn't have any cash, could you trade your car for a six-pack? What could you do?

YOUR CASH EXPENSES	COMPANY'S CASH EXPENSES

Apply the concepts to the business—where does the company get money, what does it spend it on, how much cash does the company spend in a typical day? Use the questions and answers to introduce people to the cash-flow statement.

Question to make it fun: Is a teenager with a job a source or use of cash?

Concepts, Not Statements, Are Critical

Teaching employees how to read and understand financial statements can be an important and useful element of building an open-book management process. But open-book management can't begin and end with financial statement training. After all, you are educating people to improve the business, not only to read and understand financial statements.

Providing statement training without a place to apply the knowledge is like training people on a flight simulator, but never giving them the opportunity to fly a real plane. The training might be educational—and probably eye opening—but without an end application it becomes hollow.

That doesn't mean that you shouldn't do financial-statement training. In fact, understanding financial statements is one way to begin the training process. However, for training to succeed, employees need to use the information in their daily activities.

This means breaking down the big financial statement numbers on the P&L into their component parts—critical numbers on a department-by-department level. Employees need a line of sight to the financial statements, so they can see how individual performance fits into the big picture. Along with that line of sight, they also need processes where they can use the financial information to improve the company.

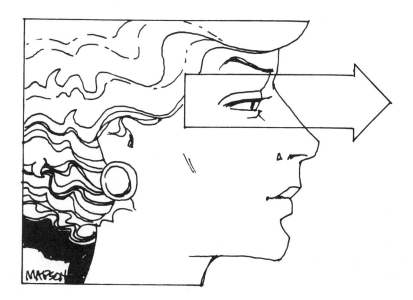

FINDING A METHOD FOR TRAINING

There are several methods to teach business concepts. Three of the most common are:

> **#1 One-on-one**
>
> **#2 Classroom training (in-house)**
>
> **#3 Outside workshops**

Since each of these approaches has its own strengths and weakness, it is important to think about how these methods will work for your company. Think of training methods you've been involved with. List the strengths and weaknesses each approach might have for your company.

	STRENGTHS	WEAKNESSES
One-on-one	_____	_____
	_____	_____
	_____	_____
Classrooms	_____	_____
	_____	_____
	_____	_____
Outside	_____	_____
	_____	_____
	_____	_____

> **Most firms use a combination of one-on-one, classroom, and outside training sources to support their business education efforts.**

SOURCES OF BUSINESS EDUCATION

When you're thinking about business education, you can use in-house resources, go outside, or use a combination of both inside and outside resources.

Business-Education Resources

IN-HOUSE	OUTSIDE
Leaders	Consultants
Huddles	Educational institutions
Peer-to-peer education	Open-book management companies
Newsletter, charts, memos	Videos, workshops, newsletters

If you're thinking about using in-house resources, ask yourself:

✔ Do the right people have the time to do it (or how can you create the time for them to do it)?

✔ Do we have the knowledge and skills in-house?

✔ Will our people listen to their co-workers?

✔ Can insiders explain their expertise in understandable terms?

If you're thinking of outside resources, ask yourself:

✔ What experience do the outside providers have?

✔ Will they customize to suit our particular needs and open-book process?

✔ Will the methods used in workshops be effective for us?

✔ Do we have the financial resources to use outside trainers?

2 VISUALS THAT ILLUSTRATE FINANCIAL CONCEPTS

People learn most effectively through interactive activities that involve them in the learning process. When you think about developing better business-people, you've got to engage people's five senses in the learning process. A mind-numbing resuscitation of the lines on the income statement is not engaging!

Research shows that 83% of our learning comes from what we see. Below are two tips on how to build interactive, visual methods to help people learn.

#1 GUESSING GAME

How are we doing on critical numbers?

Ask people to guess critical financial numbers. How much were last year's sales? How much were operating expenses, administration, interest expense, and taxes? What's our defect rate or successful shipping percent? How much did we have left in profit? How much inventory do we have? How much do our customers owe us for completed work?

Write up the guesses on a flip chart or overhead so people can see the range. When you provide the real numbers and people see how far off many of their guesses are, it will open them up to listening about the company. Many people will be surprised at how much money the company spends.

Variation: Have people write down their guesses anonymously and hand them in. Have someone read their guesses off and record them in front of participants.

#2 A HILL OF BEANS

Demonstrating the difference between sales and profit.

Take a large glass jar and put in one jelly bean or M&M for each $1,000 or $10,000 worth of sales (the bigger the jar the better). Assign roles (for example, sales commissions or scrap and rejects). Before you go through the P&L, ask participants to guess what percentage of each sales dollar is left in profit.

Go through the line items on the P&L removing the appropriate amount of candy to each expense. Once you've gotten all the way through (after taxes), lift up the jar to show how much profit is left and see how close people were on their guesses. Clearly, sales do not equal profits. Another way to do this is to print up large fake $1,000 bills, put them into a sky-high pile in the front of the room and remove them as you go through the expenses.

Variation: Print a giant dollar bill (4' × 6') and use giant scissors to cut out each expense's percentage of net sales.

MONEY TALK DOESN'T HAVE TO BE BORING

ADULT LEARNING FOR SUCCESS

When you use personal examples, hot topics, and visual media to teach employees about the business, remember that you're teaching adults. Most of us have been through numerous learning experiences in our lives, some good, some awful.

Reflect on those experiences and list below some of the factors that made the learning process successful or unsuccessful.

SUCCESSFUL LEARNING   **UNSUCCESSFUL LEARNING**

_____   _____

_____   _____

_____   _____

_____   _____

_____   _____

_____   _____

Principles of Adult Learning

In an adult-learning process, the educational process is different from our traditional instructor-pupil relationship. Principles of adult learning are:

- A focus on real-world problems and issues

- An emphasis on how learning can be applied

- Relating the subject matter to the learner's goals and experiences

- Dialogue and challenging of ideas and concepts covered

- Two-way communication: learners are resources to the instructor and each other

- Treating learners like adults: listening and respecting opinions of learners

Adults learn with games and exercises if they understand how the game is relevant. No matter how you begin your business education or who the instructors are, your chances for success will increase significantly when you use adult-learning principles.

Action Plan for Success

Use the questions below to think about how adult-learning principles will be integrated into the training process and daily conversations about the company.

How will you focus on real-world problems and issues?

_____

_____

How will you emphasize learning applications?

_____

_____

How will you relate the subject matter to the learner's goals and experiences?

_____

_____

How will you engage in dialogue and encourage participants to challenge ideas and concepts?

_____

_____

How will you ensure two-way communication and have learners be resources to the instructor and each other?

_____

_____

How will you treat learners? How will you listen and respect the opinion of learners?

_____

_____

Make sure the approach you chose is fun and engaging!

C H A P T E R

5

Developing Leadership

ADDRESSING BUSINESS CHALLENGES

"Companies that practice open-book management seem to have captured some sort of lightening in a bottle . . . Employees care about their jobs, and, perhaps even more remarkable, they care about the company."

—Training

Communication about financial information, goal setting, and business knowledge are nothing more than tools. If employees are not in an environment where they can use these tools to improve company performance and act like businesspeople, the tools will be useless and even damaging.

In a successful open-book company, the work environment encourages employees to think and act like businesspeople. Leaders no longer solve problems but instead create an environment where people can solve their own problems and tackle business challenges together. For leaders and employees alike, this may mean learning new behaviors and unlearning some survival skills that were effective in a more traditional corporate environment.

Many organizations—even those that open the books—have not been able to build an environment for working together on business challenges. At these companies, employees do not act like businesspeople. They see making money and solving problems as management's job, not theirs. Even worse, when a business challenge arises, people may hide it, try to blame someone else for it, or even ignore it. They take an approach to business issues like the one illustrated in the diagram on the following page.

ANOTHER DILLY TO COME . . .

ADDRESSING BUSINESS CHALLENGES
(continued)

*The DILLY Method**

A Common Approach to Business Problems

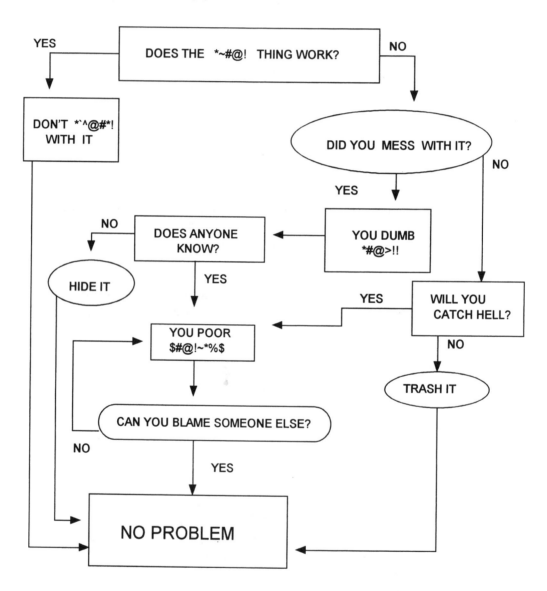

---

* The DILLY (Do-It-Like-Last-Year) Flowchart was found on a bulletin board at a large
Midwestern manufacturing facility.

Are You a DILLY Method Company?

While many people find the DILLY flowchart humorous, its usage is much more common than most leaders think. There's nothing to laugh about when you look at the results of using DILLY—business problems go unsolved, innovation is stifled, and organizations are slow to change.

Are you a DILLY company? Check all of the statements that apply to the way people take on business challenges at your company.

- ❏ Blame someone else for poor performance
- ❏ Avoid tackling problems
- ❏ When asked to participate, people say "It's not my job"
- ❏ Hide problems, rather than solve them
- ❏ People are afraid to bring up new ideas
- ❏ Work on superficial issues rather than root causes
- ❏ White knight syndrome (manager jumps in to solve all problems)
- ❏ New ideas are squelched (If it's not broke, don't fix it).

These behaviors—which were often survival skills in a traditional corporate environment—are counterproductive in an open-book environment. Open-book management requires honest talk about financial information, acknowledgment of business problems, and teamwork.

BUILDING A COMPANY OF BUSINESSPEOPLE

If people have developed some of these traditional behaviors in your company, both leaders and employees will need to learn how to work together as a team of business people. Fill in the space below to help you decide what it means to think and act like a businessperson in your company.

I'll know employees are acting like businesspeople when they:

_____

_____

_____

25 Characteristics of Businesspeople

Developing businesspeople takes time and effort. However, the rewards—for you, employees, and the company—can be substantial. Compare the list below to the actions that you wrote down.

1. Self-starters

2. Initiators

3. Problem-solvers

4. Active involvement

5. Engaged in the work

6. Working for fulfillment

7. Excited about the future

8. Committed to goals

9. Focused on the customer

10. Have a "What can I do?" attitude

11. Understand the big picture

12. Confident in their abilities

13. Willing to take risks

14. Not afraid of "thoughtful" mistakes

15. Involved in planning

16. See problems as opportunities

17. Upbeat and positive

18. Team players

19. Know the limits of their authority

20. Encourage each other to succeed

21. Know and monitor their critical numbers

22. Responsible for their performance

23. Motivate themselves internally

24. Act like businesspeople

25. Interested in how to make money

> **Building empowered businesspeople isn't something leaders do to employees. Moving from thinking like a hired hand to a business person requires both leaders and employees to change their traditional views.**

FROM HIRED HAND TO BUSINESS PERSON

*"People will act like businesspeople when
they are treated like businesspeople."*

—Steve Sheppard, CEO, Foldcraft

In an open-book management process, employees are focused on how they, in their work area, can help achieve the company's goals and objectives. In its simplest terms: what they can do to make money.

Managers no longer control the information and solve all the problems. Instead, they are responsible for creating an empowered environment. They have two key responsibilities:

#1 Building employees' skills and knowledge—particularly the connection between work and the company's strategic business goals

#2 Creating an environment where employees can use their skills and knowledge to improve the company

> **Leaders in an open-book company help people make the transition from thinking like hired hands to acting like businesspeople.**

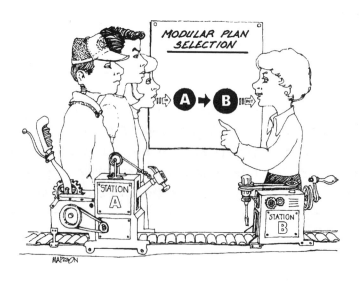

ASSESSING YOUR LEADERS

Leaders are a critical element in developing better businesspeople in an open-book company, but most have little experience in building employees' business skills or helping people make improvements.

Much has been written about the "new" supervisor and the movement from a traditional manager to an empowering coach/facilitator leader. Despite all the hoopla, most companies and leaders have made only superficial changes to their management style.

Are your leaders obstacles or catalysts of open-book management? Check all the statements below that apply to your organization.

- ❏ We hire people to do a job, not to think
- ❏ Management's job is to make the important decisions
- ❏ If people have an idea, they ought to follow the chain of command
- ❏ Supervisors are supposed to make sure people do their jobs
- ❏ Managers are responsible for customer service and quality
- ❏ Rules, not common objectives, guide our actions
- ❏ People do their jobs to please the boss
- ❏ You get ahead here by playing corporate politics
- ❏ Jobs are broken into discrete tasks to keep them simple
- ❏ Communication between departments is limited
- ❏ Managers define how jobs are done
- ❏ Each person is responsible for only his or her own job

If you checked four or more statements, you have a traditional organization. Many organizations claim that they have changed, but what they have developed resembles "hierarchy lite" more than a new workplace. Under this strategy, managers spout platitudes like, we have an open-door policy (who doesn't?) or we're a customer-focused company (who isn't?).

Employees see these superficial statements for what they are. Changes may have been implemented, but when the pedal hits the metal, leaders and employees revert to their traditional behaviors.

DEVELOPING LEADERSHIP SKILLS

A critical element of developing empowered business people is changing the traditional role of middle managers and supervisors. Because of their positions within the company, mid-level leaders are often the linchpin of any change. Their support, or lack of it, determines whether an open-book management process will fly or fail.

Leaders in an open-book environment are on a journey, moving from a traditional supervisor approach to a coaching/facilitator style of leadership. They have to build new skills to support the employees' new skills, knowledge, and role in improving the business. They need time to become comfortable with their new role of maintaining and fostering an environment that supports open-book management.

Skills of the new leader include:

- ✔ Knowledge of critical numbers
- ✔ Ability to coach rather than command
- ✔ Listening and communication skills
- ✔ Facilitating meetings
- ✔ Delegating
- ✔ Leading with vision rather than rules
- ✔ Communicating financial information
- ✔ Teaching skills
- ✔ Mentoring
- ✔ Group problem-solving skills
- ✔ Understanding of participative decision-making approaches

HOW DO YOUR LEADERS RATE?

Following is a list of characteristics of empowering open-book leaders. Rate your company's leaders on each of the statements.

1	2	3	4	5
NEVER	ALMOST NEVER	SOMETIMES	ALMOST ALWAYS	ALWAYS

	1	2	3	4	5
1. They lead with vision	1	2	3	4	5
2. View themselves as teachers, coaches/facilitators	1	2	3	4	5
3. View employees as assets	1	2	3	4	5
4. Provide constructive feedback and progressive discipline when necessary	1	2	3	4	5
5. Understand and can explain the business's goals	1	2	3	4	5
6. Feel comfortable and secure in their position with the company	1	2	3	4	5
7. Provide employees with tools and an environment to solve business issues	1	2	3	4	5

Add up all the responses. If you scored:

18 or below, your leaders need help building the skills to work with an open-book management process.

18–27, your leaders have some of the skills they need. Work with them to improve their weak spots.

28 or more, your leaders have the skills needed to get people involved in the open-book process. Encourage them to use them.

FOCUS ON BUILDING LEADERS

Look at the scale on the previous page and decide where you can focus your energy to improve your leaders' skills. Use the spaces below to list the top three areas where your leaders need improvement.

The three most important areas for improvement are:

1. _____

2. _____

3. _____

Checklist to Build Leaders' Skills

❏ **Expose your leaders to open-book management leadership styles.** Encourage leaders to visit a company that has been doing open-book management successfully. Build an internal support group for trying new skills (such as brown bag lunches). Offer reading materials. Pair leaders who are making it work with other leaders in the company.

❏ **Get leaders involved in figuring out how to make it work.** Create an opportunity for a broad cross-section of leaders (and emerging leaders) to be responsible for implementation of open-book management. Some open-book companies accomplish this by establishing a new implementation team, and others integrate it into their existing management meetings.

❏ **Provide training for new leadership skills needed.** Through seminars, conferences, and on-site training, you can provide leaders with opportunities to learn how to communicate more effectively, coach, facilitate group problem solving, run meetings, educate coworkers, and encourage employee involvement.

❏ **Teach them how to teach others about the business.** First your leaders need to know how your company makes money, then they need to learn how to teach others how it makes money.

❏ **Reward new behaviors.** Examine the items in job evaluations and incentives provided to leaders in your company. Find ways to reward and recognize leaders who are building an environment for open-book management.

❑ **Walk the talk.** Your willingness to learn to lead in a new way, admit mistakes, and be an example of the new leadership style can be the most powerful model for new leaders who need to change their approach.

❑ **Provide opportunities to practice their new skills.** Place your leaders in situations where they are asked to practice the new skills so they can learn from each other and grow.

Leadership Skills in Review

Now you have had a chance to assess where your leaders' skills are strong and where they are weak. As your leaders move from a traditional view of the workplace to a more empowering style, they take on the characteristics listed in the left column.

THEY DO	THEY DON'T
Encourage workers	Abdicate responsibility
Lead with vision	Micromanage projects
Create a supportive environment	Criticize employees in public
Help out when necessary	Take over projects
Discipline progressively	Promise what they can't deliver
Listen with empathy	Say "we tried that already"
Act as teachers	Talk down to people
Provide constructive feedback	Ignore poor performance
See employees as an asset	See employees as a cost
Work to develop their own skills	Act as a watchdog
See themselves as part of the team	See themselves as the boss
Get employee support on goals	Say "that's the way it is"
Work for creative solutions	Stick rigidly to policy
Get all employees involved	Solve employees' problems for them
Work with the team	Create a majority-rule democracy
Praise and support people	

MEASURE YOUR PROGRESS

As you know, open-book management requires you to measure your performance. You can apply this same principle to tracking your leaders' progress. Use the blanks below to help yourself, and your leaders, set clear targets.

Targets for improvement that leaders need to hit:

_____

_____

_____

_____

_____

_____

I'll know that leaders (including me) are building the environment for open-book management when I see:

_____

_____

_____

_____

6

Rewards of the
Open-Book Process

SHARING SUCCESS

"What a bonus program does is communicate goals in the most effective way possible—by putting a bounty on them."

—from *The Great Game of Business*
Jack Stack and Bo Burlingham, 1992

Imagine you invited some friends over to create a holiday feast. One contributed his family recipe for homemade bread, another brought fresh spices from her garden, and a third shared some culinary tricks from his years as a restaurant chef. As a team, you worked together to prepare a delicious dinner. When the guests sat down at the table, you loaded up your own plate and filled your glass with your favorite beverage, raising it in a toast that carefully recognized the importance of teamwork and creativity in making the meal. What would happen if you told the guests that they were not allowed to eat the food? How many of these people will help you prepare a delicious feast next year?

When you initiate an open-book process, you are inviting everyone into the kitchen. As people become more familiar with how the kitchen (business) works, they will soon see that there are rewards for creative teamwork. Sharing these rewards is an important ingredient in open-book management. Sharing rewards sends a clear message to each person that they are invited to the party as partners. Incentive rewards—properly designed—help groups work better together. In an open-book process rewards:

► **Educate people about how the business works**

► **Declare a genuine partnership**

► **Focus efforts in a common direction**

► **Help to track the group's progress**

HIRED HANDS OR BUSINESSPEOPLE?

In a successful open-book company, each person thinks more like a business-person than an employee. When businesspeople are successful, they enjoy the rewards. Successful businesspeople—whether they formally own shares or not—take ownership of the process of improving the company. They believe that their contribution will enhance the firm's performance and know that business success will be rewarding.

Getting employees to think like businesspeople is central to effective open-book management. The traditional ways people look at their contribution to work encourage thinking like a hired hand.

Rewards in the open-book process are tools for learning business-like thinking. They are vehicles for taking the journey from "hired hand" to "businessperson."

How far are people on the journey from hired-hands to businesspeople?

Which phrase describes people in your organization? Rate from 1–5 (lowest to highest) where you think most people in your company fall on the following continuum.

1	2	3	4	5
TRADITIONAL		OPEN-BOOK MANAGEMENT		

Work to please the boss   _____   Work to grow the business

Don't feel they need to know   _____   Want to know their role in big
the big picture   picture

Feel entitled to rewards   _____   Feel they earn rewards

Make choices based on short-   _____   Make choices based on long-
term rewards only   term business goals

Motivated by leadership's   Motivated by a commitment to
carrots and sticks   _____   to a common vision of future
        success

TOTAL   _____

A score of less than 15 points indicates that you feel people are closer to the hired-hand perspective than the businessperson perspective. Most organizations are here. If you are at 15 or above you think that people in your organization think like businesspeople—at least some of the time.

YOUR PLACE ON THE JOURNEY AFFECTS HOW REWARDS FIT

Without understandable shared rewards, most people will eventually choose the role of a hired hand. Choosing to be a hired hand is the path of least resistance in a traditional company; it is the work role that most of us are used to. In a fully implemented open-book management process, choosing to act like a businessperson becomes the easier path.

The design, implementation, and communication of shared rewards will depend on where you find yourself on the continuum on the previous page. The closer you are to the "hired hand" side of these continuum, the more your rewards serve as an educational tool, trust-building vehicle, and a symbol of changing roles. A start-up company needs a simple-to-explain shared reward that is tied to clearly definable group performance indicators.

As you move closer to the "businessperson" side, your shared rewards will become more of a tool for focusing employees' activities and keeping track of progress. A company in which people are regularly thinking like businesspeople can develop more elaborate reward structures. Mature enterprises may want to develop more complex reward structures to hone their focus.

REWARD STRUCTURE

HIRED HANDS	**BUSINESSPEOPLE**
Educational tool	Scorecard for our progress
Trust building	Focal point for activities
Symbol of change	Articulation of shared goals
Invitation to the banquet	Reinforces purpose

STOP. Before moving on, check your perceptions with those of others in the organization. Take an informal or formal survey asking people in your company if most employees consider themselves hired hands or partners in the business. Include top-level leaders, different departments, and informal leaders in your polling. Use the information you gather to help figure out how rewards fit into your company's open-book process.

HOW DO REWARDS HELP THE JOURNEY?

List the material rewards that employees receive at your company.

▶ _____

▶ _____

▶ _____

▶ _____

▶ _____

▶ _____

Material rewards can be fixed or variable. Fixed rewards remain fairly stable regardless of company or group performance. They include base pay, medical benefits, and retirement plans. The fixed rewards provide the security and well being that is necessary to be participants in the open-book process. Open-book companies typically set these fixed rewards at market rates or just below market rates.

Variable rewards, on the other hand, will increase and can *decrease* depending on company performance. Now, look at your list and circle the rewards that are variable. Successful open-book management companies will have both fixed and variable rewards.

Your circled incentives—which may include bonuses, profit sharing, gain-sharing, or equity ownership—take a prominent place in the open-book management process. They give workers a stake in the process of becoming businesspeople.

INVENTING INCENTIVES

Providing a stake for everyone in business success makes open-book management work. The incentives that open-book management companies use to share material rewards vary widely. Each reward approach has its own strengths and weaknesses.

Read the following examples from actual open-book companies and think about how these ideas might work in your company. Use the blanks to identify the strengths and weaknesses of each reward approach in the context of your company's current situation.

Filling Up the Bucket

A temp agency for technical professionals bases its bonus on net profits. Every time the "bucket" of profits fills to $75,000, everyone gets a bonus based on a specified share of the profits. The more times the bucket fills up, the more bonuses employees get each year.

Strengths of the approach _____

_____

Weakness of the approach _____

_____

Increasing Stakes in Meeting the Annual Plan

A medium-sized manufacturer pegs its variable rewards to meeting the annual targets set in the strategic plan. The annual bonus payout (fixed for each person) is spread out over four quarters. For example, if targets are met in the first quarter 10% of the bonus is paid. The stakes increase each quarter, 20%, 30%, and finally 40% in the last quarter.

Strengths of the approach _____

_____

Weakness of the approach _____

_____

Earn Back a Sacrifice

A steel producer set an overall target of identifying $60 million worth of cost savings. The target is reached in phases based on dollars in cost savings. As each phase is achieved, employees earn back 50 cents an hour (or a salaried equivalent) on sacrifices that they made.

Strengths of the approach _____

_____

Weakness of the approach _____

_____

Sharing Equity Through an ESOP

An insurance firm shares ownership with its employees through an Employee Stock Ownership Plan (ESOP). Each year the company makes a tax-deductible contribution to the ESOP retirement plan of 10% of compensation in the form of company stock. The value of employee accounts fluctuates with the value of the company.

Strengths of the approach _____

_____

Weakness of the approach _____

_____

MORE INCENTIVE IDEAS

INVENTING INCENTIVES (continued)

Equal Bonus Based on Customer-service Goals

An engine-parts manufacturer pays an equal bonus of $250 to all employees for any quarter in which the company exceeds its customer-service objectives. The customer-service objectives are related to the on-time delivery of product and quality goals.

Strengths of the approach _____

_____

Weakness of the approach _____

_____

Targets Trigger Annual Bonus

The annual bonus for a consumer-products distributor is paid if targets on profitability and a return on operating assets are met. Bonuses are paid as a percentage of pay. The proportion of an individual's annual pay at risk increases with increased responsibilities in the company. Percentages range from 10% of pay for hourly workers to 50% of pay for the CEO.

Strengths of the approach _____

_____

Weakness of the approach _____

_____

STRENGTHS AND WEAKNESSES OF INCENTIVES

INCENTIVE	STRENGTHS	WEAKENESSES
Bonuses tied to business targets	Can focus on more than one business indicator such as net income and cash flow	Requires knowledge and support of business goals; may be complicated to explain
Profit sharing (cash bonus based on profits)	Understandable and self-funding	Limited to a profitability measure of performance
Team/departmental incentives	Can be connected to the work that people do each day	May create unhealthy competition (better when combined with organizationwide incentives)
Gain sharing plans	Can focus on what is in employees' control	May not be self-funding and may not reflect overall business health
Individual incentives	May provide exceptional recognition	May distract from teamwork and damage the open-book process
Equity ownership (stock options, ESOP, 401(k) company stock)	Can provide a long-term perspective and encourage thinking like an owner	Does not provide frequent feedback on performance; the rewards of stock value are not immediately tangible

CHECKLIST FOR OPEN-BOOK INCENTIVES

Any reward strategy will have its own benefits and drawbacks. Organizations often combine approaches and modify them over time to reach their goals. However, open-book management incentives have some common characteristics. Check your incentives for the following qualities.

❏ **LINKED TO GROUP SUCCESS, NOT INDIVIDUAL SUCCESS—** Incentives need to be consistent with the theme of teamwork to avoid distracting employees from attaining a shared group goal. Individual targets that are independent of the group's goal can create divisions.

❏ **UNDERSTANDABLE AND EXPLAINABLE—**What can be understood easily varies over time and among companies. In most cases, this argues for simplicity in the beginning and developing more complexity over time.

❏ **TRACKED REGULARLY AND FREQUENTLY IN PUBLIC—** Regularized monitoring of the incentive (weekly or monthly) in public creates the repetition for learning and generates opportunities for improvement.

❏ **A BALANCE OF LONG- AND SHORT-TERM PERSPECTIVES—** The largest drawback of most incentives is that they can encourage short-term thinking. Many open-book companies combine equity compensation with short-term incentives to build a longer-term perspective. If you want employees to act like owners, consider making them owners.

❏ **SELF-FUNDING—**Ideally, an incentive plan does not pay out unless the company can afford it. The further a formula gets from tracking the company's overall health, the less likely it will be self-funding.

❏ **MEASURABLE AND FOCUSED ON CLEAR OBJECTIVES—** Discretionary annual bonuses are nice gifts, but they do not provide the scorecard or tool that can guide actions.

❏ **CONSIDERED FAIR AND ACHIEVABLE—**The most powerful way to achieve fairness is to provide opportunities for people to participate and have input into goal setting.

EMPLOYEES WHO ACT LIKE OWNERS

If actions speak louder than words, then equity sharing is the loudest action you can take to encourage employees in acting like businesspeople, which can be a difficult task when otherwise reasonable people believe that they are not really businesspeople. Many companies have turned to sharing equity as a way to join the long-term interests of owners and employees.

Equity sharing sends a profound symbolic message that the relationship between owners and employees has changed: people no longer are hired hands, they are business owners. Everyone is really in the same boat when employees are owners.

Practically speaking, ownership has the advantage of rewarding employees for consistent, long-term performance, rather than for short-term gains. In addition, the cash value of equity is typically realized at some point in the future, enabling the company to reinvest its cash in the business.

In more than 10,000 American corporations, employees own a significant portion of the companies where they work. Below are some of the most common mechanisms for sharing ownership.

▶ *Stock options*—Many firms are making stock options (more commonly reserved for top management) available to a broader segment of the company. These firms typically provide an option to buy stock at a price that is favorable if the company performs well. Some firms allow employees to purchase their shares through payroll deductions.

▶ *Employee Stock Ownership Plans (ESOPs)*—Company stock is held in trust for employees until retirement. ESOPs provide tax advantages for both the company and sellers in closely held firms. In addition— unlike other qualified retirement plans—ESOPs can borrow money to purchase stock.

▶ *401(k) plans*—A 401(k) pension plan can invest some of its assets in employer stock. Companies do this by contributing the employer match in the form of stock and enjoying the tax advantage of making a contribution to a qualified plan. Other firms—particularly public companies—can make their stock one of the participant's choices in the 401(k) plan.

EMPLOYEES WHO ACT LIKE AN OWNER (continued)

▶ *Direct purchase of stock*—Some firms allow employees to buy stock directly from the company. Other companies buy stock for their employees and provide it as a benefit.

Remember that stock ownership alone does not make people behave like owners. However, equity linked with an open-book process can be a powerful combination.

REVAMPING REWARDS

Do your rewards need to be modified to fit the new open-book approach? What is the next step? Some firms fashion their own bonus formula or an incentive pay system. Another option is to hire a professional to help you design an incentive plan that includes your new objectives. Whatever option you choose, remember the most important rule of thumb:

> **People will support what they help to create.**

Compensation can be a sensitive subject. Knowing what people earn and how they are paid has traditionally been the domain of only a few people in most corporations. Many leaders resist involvement in decision making about compensation for fear that it will open the door to personal agendas, manipulation, and politicking. However, without some form of involvement in the process, you run the risk of creating something that will not be effective. Incentives (even well-designed ones) are worthless if people perceive them as unfair and unachievable.

The level and type of participation each person provides will vary with individual expertise, knowledge, and level of responsibility. Most of the fears that leaders have about involving others in compensation issues can be put to rest by agreeing on the type of involvement people will have before starting the process.

Think about the groups listed below, and fill in the blanks on how you can involve them in developing compensation guidelines.

Top-level leaders _____

_____

Mid-level leaders in different functions _____

_____

Employees from different departments _____

_____

Who else should help? Who should not be involved?

REVAMPING REWARDS (continued)

WARNING! WARNING!! WARNING!!!

Be clear about the type of involvement that people take on when they are invited to participate. Are they:

- Being informed

- Providing input

- Critiquing

- Generating options

- Narrowing choices

- Being consulted

- Representing groups

- Vetoing unacceptable options

- Making the final decision?

Clarity in the beginning of the process will avoid problems later on.

TIPS FOR REVIEW GROUPS AND COMMITTEES

You may choose to establish a committee or review group to help in developing the incentive program. Below are some tips from open-book management companies on improving the effectiveness of this group.

✔ Identify the incentive's objectives before talking about any particular formulas or approaches.

✔ Ask for broad employee participation in developing the objectives and goals rather than plan specifics. Leave the specifics to a smaller, more experienced group.

✔ Use an experienced meeting facilitator from outside the organization if history, internal politics, and personal agendas are likely to inhibit the development process.

✔ If you provide options for comment or consideration, make sure that all of the options are acceptable to the company leadership.

✔ Involve the leadership of any labor organizations early in the process.

✔ Seek legal advice on labor law if the committee will be acting as a representative of employees on issues of compensation, wages, and working conditions.

✔ Get widespread agreement on a compensation philosophy that will cover everyone in the company.

✔ Link the goal setting for incentives to your strategic-planning process.

✔ Examine how well your current incentive system meets your new objectives.

✔ Weigh the negative consequences of altering your current system against the benefits.

✔ Select a professional advisor who will help you manage the participation and input process and provide expertise on appropriate formulae.

3 COMMON MISTAKES WITH VARIABLE INCENTIVES

1. PAYOUTS ARE AT MANAGEMENT'S DISCRETION

Owners or managers reserve the option of paying or not paying a bonus. Why? Because they want to retain flexibility in how they use the money. Maybe the business will run into some unforeseeable circumstance or the market will change (fill in your own reason why you need the flexibility here _____).

Employees may do the right things to earn the bonus, but management has the final say on whether it is paid. This is not a great incentive. It is like playing basketball and thinking that if your team scores the most points, you'll win, only to be informed by the referees at the game's end that the team with the most fouls wins today.

2. NO ONE CAN UNDERSTAND HOW THEY EARN A BONUS

Sometimes bonus formulas are way too complex. You've probably had one at your company before: take the return on assets, multiplied by 25% of profit after tax, subtract capital improvements, factor in this month's customer-service evaluations, minus depreciation . . . (you get the picture).

On the other hand, you might have had "Poof, the magic bonus" that appears out of nowhere, for no reason. A prime example is the Christmas bonus. Employees appreciate it, but no one understands how or why they got it. Since employees have no clue on how the bonus was earned, it has little or no effect on performance. Without a linkage to performance, it will not effect performance.

3. THE PAYOUT IS ALWAYS THE SAME

No matter what is done, everyone always earns a $1,000 bonus. The rumor is that business conditions are good, they get $1,000. The rumor is that business conditions are bad, they get $1,000. It is easy to understand why this bonus is a problem.

After a while, people view the bonus as a fixed rather than variable compensation. They feel entitled to it, rather than viewing it as something that they earn. This can lead to real human-resource problems when, for one reason or another, the "bonus" cannot be paid.

MOTIVATING WITHOUT MONEY

When you ask a person in an open-book company why they work to improve the bottom line, they will probably tell you to "get the bonus" or they might say "to make money." Similarly, if you ask an entrepreneur why they work day and night to build their business, they will likely refer to the material gains.

On the surface it looks like these people are identifying a simple truism about human nature: if you dangle money in front of people, they will work like crazy to get it. But is this really true? Is money the motivator? Consider the following contrary examples:

- Entrepreneurs who turn down higher salary jobs to run their own business

- Teams in open-book companies that regularly raise their own incentive threshold

- People who exceed the goals when the reward has already been attained

- Employees in open-book firms sacrificing material rewards in difficult times

ASSEMBLING THE PUZZLE PIECES

Contrary to myth, monetary reward is not the sole driver of the open-book process. All of the elements discussed in this book working together create the open-book environment. One element alone will not create an effective process.

Communication + Shared Goals + Business Knowledge + Leader Skills + Material Rewards = Effective Open-Book Management

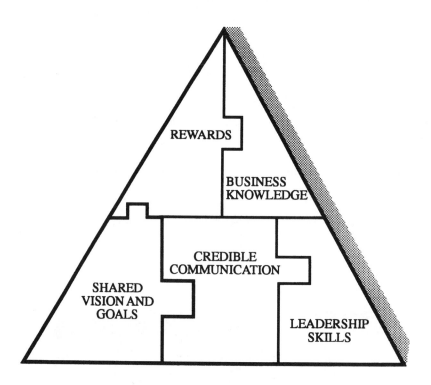

Material rewards are only one piece of the puzzle. Beyond money, the social and psychological rewards are built into the open-book process are tremendous. These rewards include: learning new knowledge, teaching others, working together toward common goals, making a difference, controlling your own future, serving the customer and your coworkers, and, of course, feeling like a winner! It is the whole process that creates these rewards.

BIBLIOGRAPHY

Bado, Jim. "Ownership Isn't a Feel Good Program," *Journey to an Ownership Culture*. New York, NY: Scarecrow Press, 1997 pp. 98–106.

Case, John. *Open-Book Management: The Coming Business Revolution*. New York, NY: Harper Collins, 1995.

Groves, Martha. "Jack Stack's Strategy to expose all aspects of finance and operation to every employee has paid off handsomely. Executives are learning the value of opening the books," *Los Angeles Times*. October 29, 1995.

Ivancic, Cathy. "Beyond Bribery: Communicating short term incentives in employee ownership companies," *Journal of Employee Ownership Law and Finance*. vol. 9 no. 1 Winter 1997.

Lee, Chris. "Open-Book Management," *Training*. vol. 31 no. 7, p. 21.

McCoy, Thomas J. *Creating an Open-Book Organization . . . Where Employees Think & Act like Business Partners*. New York, NY: AMACOM, 1996.

"Playing the game" (open-book management), *HRMagazine*. vol. 40 no. 5, May 1995.

Schuster, John P. with Jill Carpenter, *The Power of Open-Book Management*. New York, NY: John Wiley & Sons, Inc., 1996.

Stack, Jack with Bo Burlingham. *The Great Game of Business*. New York, NY: Doubleday, 1992.

Whitford, David. "Before and After (Open-Book Management at Sandstrom Products), *Inc.* vol. 17 no. 8, p. 44 (June 1995).

Webb, Cindy. "Why Johnny CEO Can't Add," *Business Week*. August 7, 1995.

Assessment

OPEN-BOOK MANAGEMENT

OPEN-BOOK MANAGEMENT: GETTING STARTED

A FIFTY-MINUTE™ BOOK

The objectives of this book are:

1. to explain the Open-Book Management process.

2. to show how to introduce employees to company financial

3. to discuss principles and techniques of adult education.

4. to provide insights into a reward system.

OBJECTIVE ASSESSMENT FOR OPEN-BOOK MANAGEMENT: GETTING STARTED

Select the best response.

1. Open-Book Management
   A. teaches employees how their companies make money.
   B. is a complicated but interesting science.
   C. must be of a unique design for any business culture.
   D. all of the above.
   E. A and C.

2. Open-book managers believe that employees can contribute best to company performance if they share in its rewards.
   A. True
   B. False

From the following list, select phrases that describe Open-Book Management to answer Question 3.

   a. sharing good and bad business news.
   b. group voting on all business issues.
   c. a right of employees.
   d. the responsibility of the Accounting Department.
   e. group responsibility for numbers.

3. Open-Book Management is
   A. a, c, d, and e.
   B. a and e.
   C. b, c, and d.
   D. b and c.

Select the best response.

4. Good reasons for a company to open its books are
   A. to empower employee teamwork.
   B. to build trust.
   C. to focus employees actions on business challenges.
   D. to increase shareholder value.
   E. all of the above.

5. The best way to provide employees with essential information for open-book management is to
   A. give frequent lectures on company financial
   B. share audited financials that go to shareholders.
   C. send key employees to college-level accounting courses.
   D. show how critical numbers affect employee work areas.
   E. make employees shareholders.

6. It is better to
   A. share all financial information at the beginning of the open-book management process.
   B. move from limited to total information as skills develop.

7. Critical numbers to share in open-book management are
   A. the same in all businesses.
   B. all company-wide critical numbers.
   C. two or three numbers that represent company goals.
   D. numbers that link to employee local goals.
   E. C and D.

8. A goal of open-book management should be to
   A. increase overtime hours company wide.
   B. decrease overtime hours company wide.

9. Having a *line of sight* to company financial provides
   A. wise decision-making by employees about use of supplies.
   B. informed employee decisions about job practices.
   C. awareness of critical links between work areas.
   D. all of the above.
   E. A and B.

10. Providing the real-time information needed for open-book management should be the responsibility of
    A. the Accounting Department.
    B. computer-based financials.
    C. people working in their jobs.
    D. management.

11. The job of Creating a company vision should rest in the sphere of management.
    A. True
    B. False

12. At the heart of the open-book management concept is
    A. communication.
    B. financial analysis.
    C. leadership skills.
    D. detailed numbers.

13. To encourage employee involvement in the open-book management process, you should
    A. present financial results in reports suitable for stockholders.
    B. find ways to make it fun.
    C. develop competition between co-workers.
    D. interpret developments for employees.
    E. all of the above.

14. Most anyone can understand business numbers if they can
    A. manage a household.
    B. understand sports statistics.
    C. plan a balanced diet.
    D. any of the above.

15. A company profit and loss statement can be compared to personal
    A. assets and liabilities.
    B. cash flow.
    C. revenue and expenses.
    D. equity.

16. The most important training for open-book management is
    A. training in reading financial statements.
    B. a line of sight from self to company performance.
    C. understanding accounting principles.
    D. keeping the complexity out of business.

17. People learn most effectively through
    A. skilled lecturers.
    B. interaction.
    C. insider training.
    D. outsider training.

18. A large glass jar full of jelly beans is a good way to show
    A. inventory related to sales.
    B. losses due to absenteeism.
    C. the difference between sales and profits.
    D. the difference between estimated profit and real profit.

OBJECTIVE ASSESSMENT (continued)

19. Adults learn best when
    A. they receive excellent lectures.
    B. learning relates to application.
    C. the lecture assumes their sophisticated skills.
    D. they can dialogue and challenge ideas.
    E. B and D.

20. Traditional hierarchical organizations that decide to introduce open-book management must
    A. create new work environments.
    B. retails successful decision-making tactics.
    C. communicate and reward new behaviors.
    D. all of the above.
    E. A and C.

21. Essential leadership skills in open-book management are
    A. coaching and delegating ability.
    B. the ability to teach group decision-making.
    C. choosing majority rule for decision-making.
    D. all of the above.
    E. A and B.

22. Rewards
    A. are not necessary in a true open-book environment.
    B. declare a genuine partnership.
    C. focus efforts in common directions.
    D. make motivation too materialistic.
    E. B and C.

23. Rewards that should be set at market rates are
    A. medical benefits and retirement plans.
    B. bonuses and profit sharing.

24. The benefit of combining equity compensation with short-term incentives is that it
    A. avoids employee short-term thinking only.
    B. balances frequent feedback with total company health.
    C. encourages empathy for all department problems.
    D. all of the above.
    E. A and B.

25. Monetary rewards
    A. are only one part of the benefit of open-book management.
    B. must combine with wise employee autonomy
    C. alone can make open-book management successful.
    D. all of the above.
    E. A and B.

Qualitative Objectives for *Open-Book Management*

To explain the Open-Book Management process

Questions 1, 2, 3, 4, 8, 9, 10, 11

To show how to introduce employees to company financials

Questions 6, 7, 12, 13, 14, 15, 16

To discuss principles and techniques of adult education

Questions 5, 17, 18, 19, 21

To provide insights into a reward system

Questions 20, 22, 23, 24, 25

ANSWER KEY

1. E	**10.** C	**18.** C
2. A	**11.** B	**19.** E
3. B	**12.** A	**20.** E
4. E	**13.** B	**21.** E
5. D	**14.** D	**22.** E
6. B	**15.** C	**23.** A
7. E	**16.** B	**24.** D
8. B	**17.** B	**25.** E
9. D		

NOTES

NOTES

NOTES

NOTES

NOW AVAILABLE FROM
CRISP PUBLICATIONS

Books • Videos • CD Roms • Computer-Based Training Products

Subject Areas Include:

Management
Human Resources
Communication Skills
Personal Development
Marketing/Sales
Organizational Development
Customer Service/Quality
Computer Skills
Small Business and Entrepreneurship
Adult Literacy and Learning
Life Planning and Retirement

CRISP WORLDWIDE DISTRIBUTION

English language books are distributed worldwide. Major international distributors include:

ASIA/PACIFIC

Australia/New Zealand: In Learning, PO Box 1051, Springwood QLD, Brisbane, Australia 4127   Tel: 61-7-3-841-2286, Facsimile: 61-7-3-841-1580
ATTN: Messrs. Gordon

Singapore: 85, Genting Lane, Guan Hua Warehouse Bldng #05-01, Singapore 349569   Tel: 65-749-3389, Facsimile: 65-749-1129
ATTN: Evelyn Lee

Japan: Phoenix Associates Co., LTD., Mizuho Bldg. 3-F, 2-12-2, Kami Osaki, Shinagawa-Ku, Tokyo 141   Tel: 81-33-443-7231, Facsimile: 81-33-443-7640
ATTN: Mr. Peter Owans

CANADA

Reid Publishing, Ltd., Box 69559-109 Thomas Street, Oakville, Ontario Canada L6J 7R4.   Tel: (905) 842-4428, Facsimile: (905) 842-9327
ATTN: Mr. Stanley Reid

Trade Book Stores: *Raincoast Books,* 8680 Cambie Street, Vancouver, B.C., V6P 6M9   Tel: (604) 323-7100, Facsimile: (604) 323-2600
ATTN: Order Desk

EUROPEAN UNION

England: *Flex Training,* Ltd. 9-15 Hitchin Street, Baldock, Hertfordshire, SG7 6A, England   Tel: 44-1-46-289-6000, Facsimile: 44-1-46-289-2417
ATTN: Mr. David Willetts

INDIA

Multi-Media HRD, Pvt., Ltd., National House, Tulloch Road, Appolo Bunder, Bombay, India 400-039   Tel: 91-22-204-2281, Facsimile: 91-22-283-6478
ATTN: Messrs. Aggarwal

SOUTH AMERICA

Mexico: *Grupo Editorial Iberoamerica,* Nebraska 199, Col. Napoles, 03810 Mexico, D.F.   Tel: 525-523-0994, Facsimile: 525-543-1173
ATTN: Señor Nicholas Grepe

SOUTH AFRICA

Alternative Books, Unit A3 Micro Industrial Park, Hammer Avenue, Stridom Park, Randburg, 2194 South Africa   Tel: 27-11-792-7730, Facsimile: 27-11-792-7787
ATTN: Mr. Vernon de Haas